It Can Be Solved By Walking

"In this collection of poems and photographs, Jennifer Wallace blends two of the humanistic art forms to capture glimpses of her adopted city of Baltimore: its history, its pride, its squalor, its nature, and its people. With acute observation, robust description, and artful wit, she invites us to view the neighborhoods of Baltimore at a walking pace without preconceptions or illusions as to what cities are supposed to be. She cherishes the ordinary, the vernacular, the sordid, and the humane faces of cities without judging them. This is a wonderful contribution to a new humanistic understanding of cities."

Rutherford H. Platt

Professor of Geography Emeritus, University of Massachusetts Amherst

Editor, *The Humane Metropolis: People and Nature in the 21st Century City*

"Jennifer Wallace's poems explore a unique landscape where finely tuned observation and visionary imagination come together in endlessly surprising ways. Through graceful verse and haunting photographs, Wallace sets out to create a psychoecology of city and country, showing how they interact in mysterious dances of similarity and difference. During the journey she discovers something still more marvelous, an ecology that embraces both the human senses and what can only be called the soul of modern life."

David Sterritt, Ph.D.

Chief Book Critic, *Film Quarterly*

Chairman, National Society of Film Critics

Co-Chair, Columbia University Seminar

"Baltimore can be a difficult city — and an even harder one to put down on paper. As Jennifer Wallace writes, one must be 'in love with the difficult stories / because they are not mine, because they are mine.' Her rich poems and photographs perfectly capture the sights, sounds, and flavors of the city's urban ecology. Truly the amazements of her book are what come not only by walking, but also from seeing with clear and compassionate eyes."

Reginald Harris
10 Tongues
Finalist, Lambda Literary Award

"Jennifer Wallace works way out at the very edges of form — in environmental terms, at the ecotone, that transitional zone where two habitats meet, mingle characteristics, and shelter creatures who thrive on varieties of sustenance and protection, and changing, dappled light. So just what is this gorgeous work — a poetic essay? travel journal? city daybook? collection of reading notes? photojournalistic sequence? Amazingly, all these inclinations find a place within. A passionate attachment to the heartbeat of language, the ambling rhythms of a city walker, and bone-clean lines shape these meditations and are the means by which Wallace sifts Baltimore's grief and beauty, its land- and humanscape, for gold."

Lia Purpura
Author, *On Looking*
Finalist, National Book Critics Circle Award

Library of Congress Control Number: 2012932936
ISBN: 978-1-936328-05-5
CityLit Project is a 501(c)(3) nonprofit organization
with offices in the School of Communications Design
at the University of Baltimore.
Federal Tax ID Number: 20-0639118

Printed in the United States of America | First Edition
Cover and Book Design: Laurie Pagano
Author Photograph: Judy Remmel
Cover Photograph: Jennifer Wallace

c/o CityLit Project
120 S. Curley Street
Baltimore, MD 21224
410.274.5691
www.CityLitProject.org
info@citylitproject.org

It Can Be Solved By Walking

Jennifer Wallace

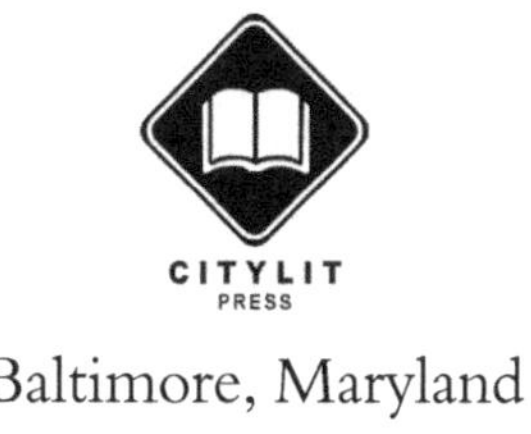

Baltimore, Maryland

Contents

[. . .]

It Can Be Solved By Walking

Tell me what you know

Tell me what you know and don't know.
I will, too. Knee to knee, let's sit
among the seasons and nebulae.
Among colossal pinpricks: an emptiness.
And in those cold waters, we'll moor
our separate boats in the other's company,
wander the continents, each country, our cities,
the fields we rolled in, and where – one day –
we'll lay ourselves to root again.

North Avenue and Broadway East

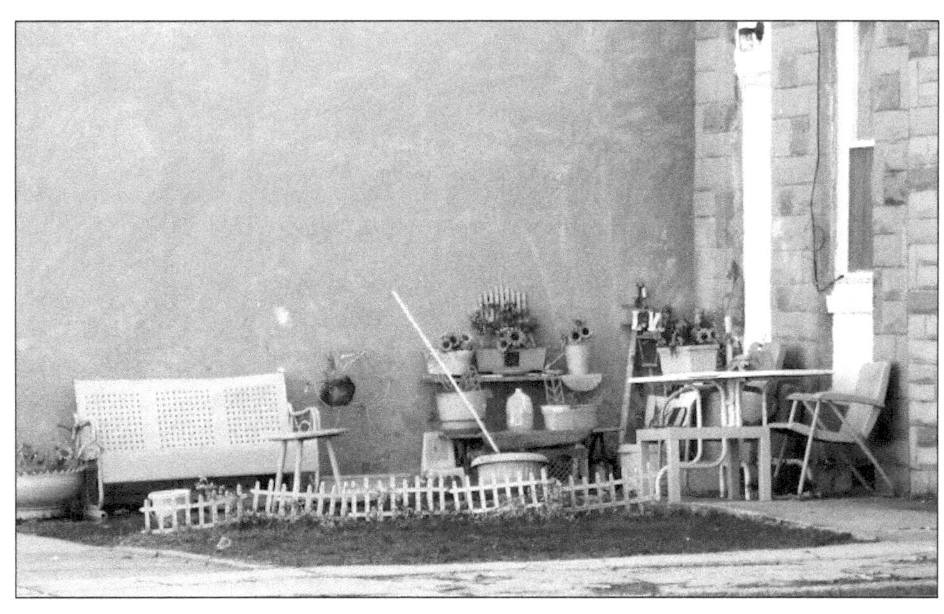

I wanted to change my name

I wanted to change my name, find a remote island
off the Newfoundland coast. The only way to get there would be by boat,
and only I would send it and only on occasion. I'd be a friend
of gannets. Emerson's new protégé.

Time would exist as it should: tidal and thick as a forest.
I'd be historical. A spinster on a bright day clipping asters outside
a clapboard shed, my graying hair wild with wind. In November,
I'd split wood and welcome the kid from town who'd deliver my mail.
I'd catch my fish. I'd be a kingdom, an ecology.

How could I have known that my arrival would build itself
on contradiction. Instead of ocean: murder; exhaust, not flowers.
In this metropolis: all the homes with the name "Stranger"
carved on their doors.

There is a grammar etched in the mind's bone. A topography
that can be counted on. It might erode — with time and weather — but beauty
and ugliness run in its gullies. With more or less volume. At will, if willed.

The lake sits flat today

The lake sits flat today.
Citizens of my new city circle it. Most of them are black.
I watch. They jog, walk, pedal, skate.

I know about lakes,
having come from the northern suburbs
where they are blue-green and numerous.
A blue-green landscape and shining,
where clouds float across the lakes like birds,
where white organized everything. White,
a blanket, a color, a shroud.

I've arrived in Baltimore, blue-green and ignorant.
I watch my neighbors' dailiness, circling. Their reliable strangeness.

What is familiar? Not a place, a people,
but movement — each day the people circling. The gulls.
Like bits of cloud, they identify the air.
Air, inclusive, wrapping the city in great sheets of light.

My neighbors circle the lake in their colorful outfits.
The man in the red shirt who walks while reading a book.
The old woman with the too-big cap goes twice around.
A mother pushes a stroller as a herring gull breaks for a fish.
Her child points at them and yells: "Look!"

Reliable as weather, the corner

Reliable as weather, the corner
glitters with grit while citizens
wait for the bus and pick
lake trout from their teeth. A man
with Ziplocs meets a woman and her kid.
She gets her stash. This pocket, a stillness.
Those who lean
under the orange sign: *Chicken Nook, Chicken Nook* —
the throbbing glow of it.

I startled a peregrine

I startled a peregrine while walking near the station.
First winter days. The pewter sky.
A vacant lot with leafless trees, gray limbs.
The bird that flew from there with something in its claws,
dangling and also gray.

The city shudders in the difficult wind.
A train rumbles through the tunnel.

The bird was quiet and I was;
the rat or the pigeon
tucked snug against its belly.

Glad for the peregrine.
Glad for the city.
Poor rat. Poor pigeon.

A train in the station.
All the travelers on their way.

His orange rig at the iced-in curb

His orange rig at the iced-in curb.
Deep under there
the city's pipes have cracked.

One boot two rungs down the hole,
another propped on the rim.
His breath steams, then stops —
as he lets the ladder go.

His ordinary work.
His return from earth to earth.

City roofs at night under snow

City roofs at night under snow
their peaks
and the calm clouds fallen…
Under them: a family. A widow. One home
whose eyes are dark.

The snow holds the multiple lights.
A halo. Imagine: over their various lives.

In another season

In another season,
a train, distant, with a mournful horn
opening the day: overcast but full of birds.
Their industry, and the crickets
and cars whizzing the avenues.

My chair, rooted in grass blades,
a place to depart from sleep. I am
that sparrow on the alley wire. And the sirens —
even at this hour. Even in this calm.

Particulars, holy and minute

Particulars, holy and minute,
right here, in the bookstore café
where the women gossip and chew
and the man with the green hat
props his bandaged thumb
in the book he soon might own.

Muffin crumbs under the table on the red tiled floor.
A hair strand tinseled on the chair's rung
and Otis Redding's hum under the milk steamer's whiz.

This is the world: animate with the intricate.

The door opens and closes
and a deep field arrives in t-shirt and jeans.
Outside: the storefront
with its warm yellow light, lonely as Hopper's,
and a source we believe but cannot see.

The soft hum of these bugs

The soft hum of these bugs is paradoxical against the city's brick.

And in an instant — my white Keds scuff through the vacant lot
next to our half-built house…the buzz and crackle, hum and click
of insects in the scrub.

I never liked it. The sound is poor. Dirt poor and menacing.
A menacing naturalness I thought was long gone. Instead, the memory
wedges between these row homes, fills the narrow lot between them.
The creamy steps worn-in from the soles of so many leavings.

My own nomadic family left every four years for a different town, often
in different states. And the places — laden with difficulty. I had a childhood.
We played in parks. I learned to row a boat. But no one talked. We
didn't think. There was a lot of drinking. Stuff happened. This is not
important except for what it left: the impulse to track down, figure out,
to connect.

'The meaning of the word — here — contains the meaning of oneself.'

If so, then I am here…in front of these row homes…on the move…
in the insect-clicking city, with a terrible need to read the points of exchange,
the pathways, the gaps. A natural system of movement toward gathering.

The point being: a particular history contains and is contained,
makes itself known and, through me, touches the weight of footprints on stone.

[. . .]

The guy who wanders under the highway. The tire traces
in sand. The woman whose posters beg for something to explain
her daughter's death. An old lady on the stoop. Her stuff. The ant,
mockingbird. Trains and their rails. Each of these: nodes of meaning
that river their way through the city, make it a place of belonging
and unbelonging.

The insects are near to me and near me to the world.

Roofline –

Roofline —
where pigeons study the intersection of Aisquith and North.

A particular building
the particular intersection
          bus stop, gasoline
          burgers and ribs
evidence of

two species
at rest, a red light
20 drivers : 20 birds

incomplete in our differences, our likenesses.

The tarpaper sun trap.
The asphalt sun trap.

A need for, commonplace.

The small minds: pigeon-sized.
Oily feathers, opalescent in the January sun.

Sirens gust beyond the rooftops

Sirens gust beyond the rooftops.
Vacancy beyond those rooftops,
the murderous sidewalks not far from home.

Deshawn (in the news) said:
        "I would change the story…a quiet part of town
        where knives and guns fall asleep while we play."

Baltimore's poverty weaves itself across the avenues.
Its achievements cross-stitched, plot line
punctuated by small trees
in small sockets. An ecology.

'Whether we like it or not, humans
have become the meaning of the earth.'

My eyes look everywhere

My eyes look everywhere: needles and neon, a few squirrels.

Sometimes I withdraw from the city. Not kneeling toward
the moss rock by the sea. And all the while the seasons rush over
the sidewalks: petals, colored leaves, the neighbors' footfalls. Crows
flock to the parks, gather in the trees. The closeness of otherness is touching
but not to be touched.

. . .

I am asked: "Do you think living in the city has something to do with
your poems about thought?" As in: will a place that bends the rain
make things more clear? As in: a man talked to his son about
the bird's obsessive flight: in and out of the chimney's narrow passage…a dumb
flight that must be undertaken: 'It is deeper than your father, boy.'

. . .

On street corners: a handshake, fist, words exchanged. The fears
excited by such intimacies. Are momentary. Replaced by: "Which bus
is mine?" And we are on our way. To the parks and gardens, which
present an illusion of access.

Today at the corner, a lady dressed all in green…new-leaf green…
green shoes, even, against the concrete curb. We were looking for
a bus in the rain. Pelting rain, all over those shoes. Impenetrable,
natural rain. She carried Jehovah's pamphlet. We were looking.

There's conflict about a pigeon's worth

There's conflict about a pigeon's worth.

Twenty gargoyles roost on the ledges,
the city's richest citizens thrive on scraps and bones.

Their most vigorous defense: a tail spread, gaped bill
                                        a strike with a lifted wing.

They do fine in artificial light.
And don't mind the ridicule
of those who struggle to survive.

. . . an angular aspect to the city

…an angular aspect to the city. A person can be at home
in such seriousness. The streets receive her and she fills them, fills herself
with them. And the warm light pours from the street lamps,
makes a way; the danger in the alleys gives way. A sort of fierceness emerges
as she walks between the lights. A fierceness that may
run counter to the civilized image. But survival is civilized. Power
pervades it. The lamps flood the place with vision, which is power.
And the people gather there.

. . .

My heart goes out to them. So many items in the carts they haul.
Their kids holding on. I remember that my sons loved the subways.
The excitement between the tracks and the "plug-our-ears" rumbling.
I kept them from under the wheels. The city was a danger. Going there,
an excitement, a sign of our wealth.

. . .

One morning, early, I saw a woman and her stroller. She was a few
yards away from the stroller and followed something on the sidewalk…
far, too far from her baby. She looked down and
shuffled around, frantic. This was strange behavior for a mother: close
to the street, far from the stroller. I asked if I could help and she showed me
the rabbit, tawny with white ear tufts. A wild rabbit huddled
against brick. "They escape from the university labs," she said.
"At this time of year there are so many of them…they stray across the avenue."

[. . .]

She said if I caught it she'd take it to the shelter. She used her stroller
to herd it. I tried and tried to catch the rabbit, tried to throw my sweater
over its head and the woman tried to pin it against the wall.
Finally it hopped behind a dumpster in a parking garage.
A natural reaction, not wanting to be saved.

. . . a place wedged between

        ...a place wedged between the tracks and the interstate. Between
the towers and the run-down shacks. Down in the dross-place, the gully
        that was once a valley, that was once a trace before its carving.
Long ago...too long to be remembered, but remembered.

        Its tunnel — engineered to save the citizens from themselves, to transport
the river better than it could transport itself. Underground.
        Driven under. The river driven into the city's mouth.
Expertly crafted by masons. It accepts the river, routes it. A monumental
        achievement.

        A person can cross the guard rails, go down among the water
and stones. Among the sad bottles, small bags used up in someone's loving.
        A person can kick through the meaning of what's left there and
of the water's flow.

        When I was a child I explored creek beds in California, I was eaten
by an imaginary whale in Illinois. I kicked rocks on the drought-stricken
        shores of Kentucky's Cumberland Lake. I pretended to be
a scientist. I *was* a scientist with my little bony knees and my brother-partner,
        who held his glasses together with first aid tape. What we found
wasn't the polished magic of museum store geodes. Ours were
        dirty and dull. But in those moments, I cracked open, too. Exposed,
dull (probably) but to myself: a fascination.

[. . .]

Here, walking with the river, which — without stopping —
flows under the homes and tall buildings, I am fascinated, still, and carry
inside myself the earlier footsteps; carry the stories Cleo told me:
"After the flood, they found a body down there." The stories drip
from my feet like fingerprints.

Inventory

Delivery (five cases per hand truck)

Tanned, muscular, sweat beads roll like raindrops across his tattooed chest.

Sparrows and razor wire

A young woman on a window ledge under them; her face buried in her arm.

Reward

"For a reliable witness: $5,000 to anyone who knows about the accident that killed my daughter."

Exchange

Under the highway, two guys at a pick-up truck. After work? Before sex?

Cleo

Old woman in a ski cap in August at rest in her square-of-a-yard. Blue tablecloth spread out for her wares.

Flashback, Stone Hill (Mt. Vernon Mill Co., circa 1840)

A shirtless black man walks the dirt path among those stone houses.

Gang

Street kids, breast milk still on their cheeks. Too young for the coded shapes implied by their hands.

[. . .]

Leavings

Denim hung high from the maple limb. Cuffs rolled, bicycle locked to the sapling trunk;
co-ed's high-heels: one already off the curb.

Roosts

Tent under the overpass/starlings among the wires above the tracks/apartments:
opem and half-built where the workers bang and clap and the birds fly in.

Histories

At the college, train cars speed past the Buddha's raised arm.

At Rest

Grizzled man with his cane. Serious gargoyle on the bench.

Along the River Way Back When

Alberton Cotton Mills, James S. Gary & Son, Osnaburgs, Twills, Denims, Cotton Warps,
Carpet Chains and Awning Stripes in Fancy Colors, Green, and Alberton Blue.

Baltimore Sun, August 25, 1871, Ross Winans

"Even now the best interests of the city would be served by taking immediate measures to store up and control the entire waters of this stream. The number of families…using baths in their houses should be increased…in European countries the laboring classes practice bathing more than here…"

[. . .]

Lock

Fingers figure the key to what is meant to keep them out.

Petals

Strange gathering. Uncollectable in April's wind.

October 28, Mount Royal Avenue

Two bald eagles low enough to see their legendary heads above where we sit.

Accordion Man

Picturing him. 'Made of so many things.'

Tomatoes

Even against chain link, their globes promise sustenance.

Moment

It could mean a sidewalk. A snapshot. It could mean an alleyway
or the interval between footsteps. The distance between mind and chest.

How do I know myself, this place?

How do I know myself, this place? My place — the space
of my knowing?

Lofty ideas…the way the snow drifts and lofts, full of moisture
and air. Wind and clouds aloft, above the movements of the city's people.

There are actual buildings where we rest and argue. Mrs. McDonald
puts a kettle on. Mr. Jamal cuts some hocks. Thinking thoughts.
Remembering to do something later. Remembering another time
when someone older taught them to boil and cut.

And when I go out onto the sidewalks I notice ice, wet shoes.
The day will be nasty. I know it and carry it like a satchel all day. The way
information weaves through the streets and markets, among
the parishioners — but vaguely — the same way the news about icebergs
and disease makes its way. The one Ms. Krynski takes a pink pill for.
The one everyone knows about but can't change.

The snow piles up and changes everything. The trees, rooflines,
roadways — all of it inconvenient, cold and new. Wonderful. The way
cider steam swirled above the pot that day they cancelled school.
Brothers and sisters, kids from next door. A tent made of blankets. A parent
or a friend's parent yelling and laughing.

In the snow, a warmth to the streets without their trucks and buses.
The city, now unknown, takes me — aloft. A kind of disclosure.
As when a cloud flake hits my tongue.

In love

In love
because the city won't let up
no matter how much rocking.
In love with this city
as if a surprise walked through the door
wearing suspenders and red-striped pants.
In love with the intersection
and its ingenious abutment of asphalt and grit
where chicory roots in their joining
and age-old rainwater bubbles in the gutter
bobbing toward the harbor and the sea.
In love with the difficult stories
because they are not mine, because they are mine.
The just-after-dawn light
like Caravaggio's on the row house bricks.

A mind surveys the rooftops

A mind surveys the rooftops.
Wires crisscross the alleyway.

A squirrel on the wire running,
Furred claws curled around electric weavings.
It runs between the shingles and the trees.

Is it *running*? Or something more squirrel-like —
Not: "I want that walnut," but something
squirrel-voiced or voiceless.

A mind can't know what it is.

The concrete actual

The concrete actual

an actual gunshot

a fashionable restaurant

the operatic unemployment line

the rat and starling run free.

Look for the original river,
underground. Still. In its culvert.

Pooling the harbor, reservoir. The pipes
animated and quenching.

A faint and cacophonous entanglement.

At the station

At the station, passengers enter the city
carrying their stories on their backs:
the time when one skinned a knee
or when the other first listened to Bach
or the one whose ancestor birthed the master's child.

Their footfalls, soft against the sidewalks.
They inhale a new world; it feeds them.
Each out breath amplifies the streets.
The pigeons perch in trees growing with their memories.

When the orange disc hoists itself

When the orange disc hoists itself into the day
the beer-bottle stream glitters. The early ones
drive to work, another walks her dog. A routine.

But this morning, I'm surprised to remember:
the sun doesn't really rise. The rainstorm
with its Kansas winds; the robins —
back from Belize — exist
because the earth is axis-bound and turning; and somehow —
atop all its birth and murder — a mother
makes lunch for her kid; he's late for school
and pedals fast against time's curve.

Whatever might be said or known — we are hurling
cold and full of tender sand and color. Look!
The bright shoulder on the black bird's wing.

On that day a sea wind

On that day a sea wind
grazed the graveyard hill.
What was left of Isabel
tracked north toward Canada. And I sat still,
above east Baltimore, with my back
against the stones, against the clouds.
There's something strong about the oldest
markers, off-kilter, pushed up and over,
unphased by the earth's sure moving .

Across town, south and west, but also
on a hill looking eastward toward the bay,
Mt. Auburn's stones are tended
by the neighbors when they have some time.
The sign marker calls it
"City of the Dead for Colored People" —
since 1868, after their land-rooted sweat,
the only place in town where the freed slaves rest.

The winds blow from that direction.
I'm sure the storm swept through there first,
reminding me there is no end to the battering,
no north and south, no difference between east and west.

One lives in a world

One lives in a world
is lived in by a world
punctuated by robins and jackhammers
containing an innerness bigger than its skin.

A train crosses the night city —
its horn calls out for something, while the pigeon huddles,
while the citizens sleep.
It could carry televisions.
It was one of the horrible trains.
It could be an escape route.

See what the world is like?
A grammar without language
but striving for language.
Endangered if not actual, if not spoken of.
Becoming a virtual place
where no one is close, no one is far away.

Imagine: An ocean. No, bigger.
A universe? No. A bridge
still being built. In search of bedrock,
in search of its actual shores.

The world outside the body is large

The world outside the body is large, much larger than the body,
contained as it is by bones and skin. The body, alone, takes a whole day
to traverse the city and in that crossing: so many people,
rows and rows of stoops and steps.
Downtown: monuments. More than one person selling something.
So many spires, bells. A few trees and grass blades, the reservoir,
the grand park with its gazebos, clock towers, alley cats
and daffodils in their tended beds. Rain falls from an enormous sky.

. . .

I used to sit at the seashore watching the big waves get smaller
and the small crabs and the places on the sand where the waves unrolled
to their last tiny curling. I wondered if this foamy nothing was,
to the crab, as the large wave was to me.

. . .

What if one day, waking equaled a set of new landmarks. Instead
of rumbling intersections, there would be windows. Taxis would present
their mysteries...the river that subverts the grid would continue
underground, while its tunnel opened to us.

[. . .]

A long time ago humans invented civilization without knowing it.
It wasn't like electricity or the telephone, where someone said,
"What a good idea!"...No, a couple of tribes with a few goats
discussed the advantage of staying together in order to save whatever water
could be gathered in a drought. And now: some of us are learning
how to die in our own beds. Enough of us are wondering together
and many to ourselves.

. . .

What if Rilke approached and offered you a small bird.
His right hand, close to yours and the bird's too-thin legs dangling
between his fingers. The bird's belly is nested in his hands, so
it is obviously happy there, but Rilke is willing to disturb all that. He said:
the world is unfinished until it enters you.

. . .

The world outside is large. But the world inside our limited frames
is where the shop owner becomes. The alley cat goes backwards to its
lion days. In us, the avenues and museums are only ideas growing
toward the inventions they will become.

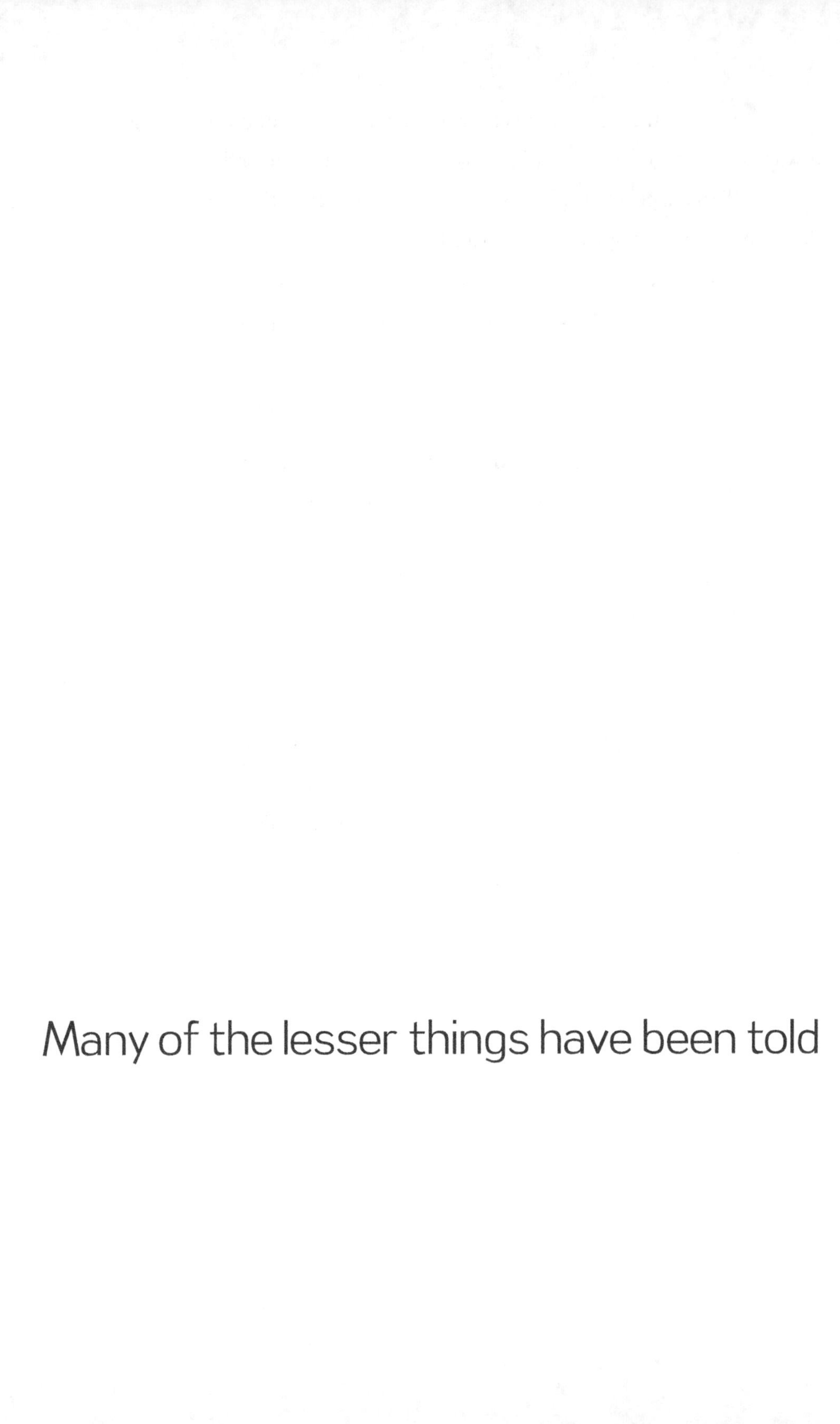

Many of the lesser things have been told

'Many of the lesser things have been told:'
pyramids, the Great Wall, a glass eye into the deep field.
A few odd bones in an African gorge. Footprints
found on the rim, turned westward.

But the greater things have not been told:
what they thought when they looked at it —
what each of them thought (they were not common yet).

So much is missing. The story of their tracings —
there and on the city stoops — imaginable
but unfinished unless imagined — the evolution, for example,
of compassion technologies. As in:
one chimp grooms another after the bonds of attack.

Someone, somewhere still digs

Someone, somewhere still digs with her hands, another walks barefoot
to his daughter's school. Somewhere a body grows because of seedlings
that were helped through a frost with ungloved hands.

. . .

While refugees on all continents are in "no place," they walk together
to the next encampment, which is "no place" too, and maybe is
made into something with their dancing, which can't be
easily understood. 18 million feet together and alone, pounding the earth.

. . .

In America, everything lasts except the citizens. The idea of them
lives as long as stories are told: the earth-worn settlers, the earlier mothers
used their sticks to plant corn. But I am not one of these and will not last
as long as the sullied rivers that flow and flow.

. . .

It is impossible to attend to the whole world. And that is an embarrassment
and an anxiety. That I am part and therefore partial. Forgetful of what's fleeting.
A singular engine of fleetingness. Matter flows and energy cycles,
so say the newest texts.

. . .

When speaking a foreign language: grammar is clear but not
the meaning. I travel anyway: excited by and tense with this awareness.

I study the lake's light

I study the lake's light
as it rises pink against blue.

On days with small winds,
its face wrinkles; big storms
capsize the shore reeds
and drive the gulls away.

Here, I learn about the collegiality of flocks;
I love the dips and arcs they make.

'What landscape paints itself in me?'
My own singularity stands out, bone-deep.

First of all you will fail

First of all you will fail; it can't be seen.
Heisenberg proved that
it can be measured using two equations
but how does that work? Two —
two truths, two of the same truth.

We see the tree's upward branching
and say: look at the gingko in the park,
its fan-shaped leaves. Ancient. Look at them fall
all at once. An unusual truth, among trees.

Unless we dig way down
and wide as the crown
we don't see the roots
or the water pockets they search for.
In cross-section we may have seen them
(and this because a botanist dug one up).
We may have seen
a tree uprooted by a strong wind, the wide spread of the under branches
those that wind their way under the pavement. Those
boulder-tangled. With their miniscule hairs. The growth tips
bounced upon by trucks and vans.

[. . .]

And on the hot sidewalks, unusually hot, too hot,
we walk and worry. The man with a gun. The stray with one leg.
The daughter: knocked up. The mother and father. Someone
with a broken gene.

A song from the accordion on a park bench mixes with all this.
Too much of it. The deep striving. The crown also striving.
And a finger-sized goldfinch, a yellow blast
zipitty-zip between the trees.

I never get tired

I never get tired of cogitating. There are so many things I'd like to know.
And knowing them would solve so many problems — the small ones:
like whether or not humans have become the meaning of the earth
and the large ones: like whether the word 'here' contains the meaning of myself.

If 'one truth moves from the inside and one from the outside
and when they meet we see ourselves,' then I can see a dense muscle
pumping against its hollow core; that fist-shaped organ —
how it beats and beats its delicate wings.

It can be solved by walking

It can be solved by walking
or take a bike.
Something slower than driving.
Something less contained, especially. Something
that permits a breeze or a squirrel to enter, a rat
to rattle you — that sort of surprise
the kind that's overruled by 'the speed and strength
that is the armor of the world.'

Unplug the ears.
The honks and screeches roll in like Mozart. Unbuckle
the distaste for poverty and grit.

The world is either a beautiful iceberg
or a mountaintop
thrown from its source to the faraway sea.
And the gods, who aren't believed in any more, are out there hiding
behind windows, under the stoops.

One of them struts the sidewalks with his two-colored hat.
One side of the street sees red. The other side, green.
He passes again with his hat flipped around just for fun.
Everyone goes to court. It's a kind of togetherness.
All of us arguing and 'shining like the sun.'

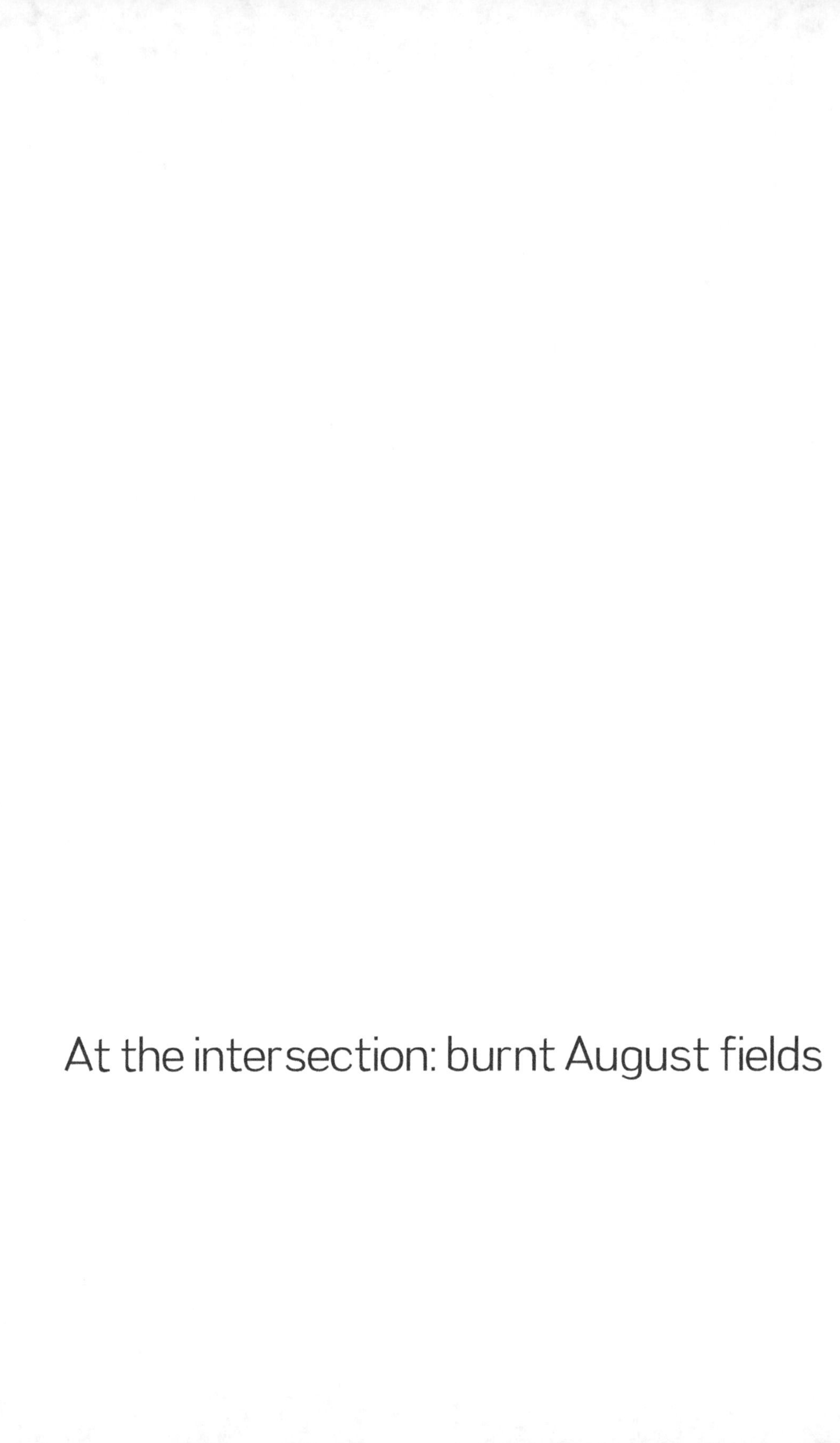
At the intersection: burnt August fields

At the intersection: burnt August fields and blistered streets.
The city readies for summer's last fling.
Vendors circle the band shell
with curried goat and Red Stripe beer. The sound man
"check, checks" his mics and Marley's wail unites
with insect wings and chicken smoke and air.

Where is Jamaica? Baltimore? Where?
Tonight they reside on music's continent —
behind the chain link, where holstered cops
keep peace between the races
who don't appear to need much help…
they boogie bum to bum under the moon
and all the colored lights and everyone singing *One Love*.

There were people down in the depths

There were people down in the depths and they didn't know
they were people. One of them broke a taboo that nobody knew was taboo
and the floodwaters rushed in. They had to get out; they used a rope
that they threw from below, through a hole above, and into the city of the world.

When they climbed out, they were in another world. Someone in power
insulted the sun and moon, so everyone was in the dark. The priests said, "O,
we can get it back" and so they swallowed the plants and trees but everyone
was still in the dark.

Then the animals were allowed to try; they made a circle and danced
and danced some more and danced until a hill started to grow out of which
all the others came.

And everyone was surprised to see those others, who looked like them,
but were not them.

We seek a form, a shape

We seek a form, a shape — adequate enough: the kitchen table, mother's leg —
the thing to hoist ourselves. Barely arrived, we already aim for the sun.

Piling our maple blocks, we are makers from the start. A log laid across the stream,
the bark boat with its leaf sail, a ladder to a platform in the pines. Something

makes us want to cross, to climb. Something we are born with
invents a larger lens, metal wings, rockets. We scheme.

Our plans — torn and pasted — made, remade. The secret covered, uncovered
and covered again. Higher, ever higher. To be grazed by the hawk's wing; fed,

like Elijah, by the ravens' horny beaks. A vigil, and whatever we might surmise
about blue-black space, the limits of what we see.

What is wished for? To be tree-like, god-close? Outside of time?
We are preoccupied with prominence. The point, through whatever haze or light,

always farthest from "what is." It's not enough to see the sun and stars,
but to *be* one of them. Or beyond, the furthest place. Something in us *knows*

there's something we must find. If only we could find the form, build the thing.
What kind of wood? How many steps? Where to tie the ropes? Spindly or spired?

And the other ones, those we make with hope or the nails of loss and grief…
the thing through which, with which, we might arrive above our flesh and blood,

[. . .]

above the moss, outside of air. Would it be benevolent? Malign?
A place we don't need eyes to see. Unfixed, unlike the towers we make to get us there.

A place to startle us. As in love's moment. Would we let down our guard? Forget
who or what we seek? We would arrive at the deepest eye, the one

that would let itself be entered, be taken in and taken. What would we, then,
what could we, name the seeker? The carrier of thought and all its structures?

What is known — at last: a certain rust and beetle-bitten ruin, the sure return
to all we've ever feared or dreamed.

From within

From within
From within the egg
From within the egg of the world
'From within the egg of the world I pierce the shell,
then I see the face of necessity...'

Palm pressed
from within the chalky shell
from within:
            the faintest   field of weakness,
the inevitable peck, peck, peck
and then the light, the bewildering light.

Dickson Street and W. Lafayette Avenue
Bolton Hill

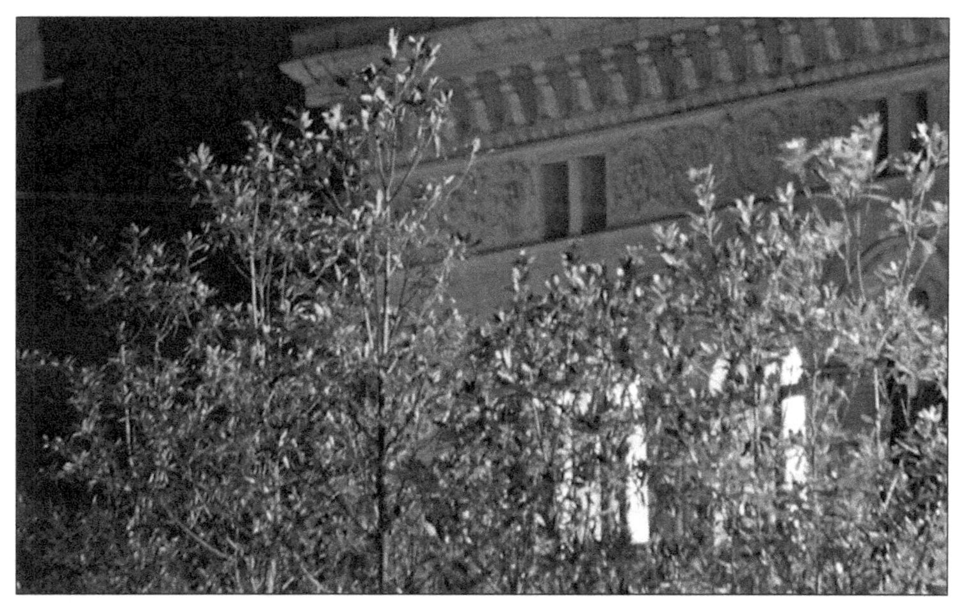

Dickson Street and W. Lafayette Avenue

Bolton Hill

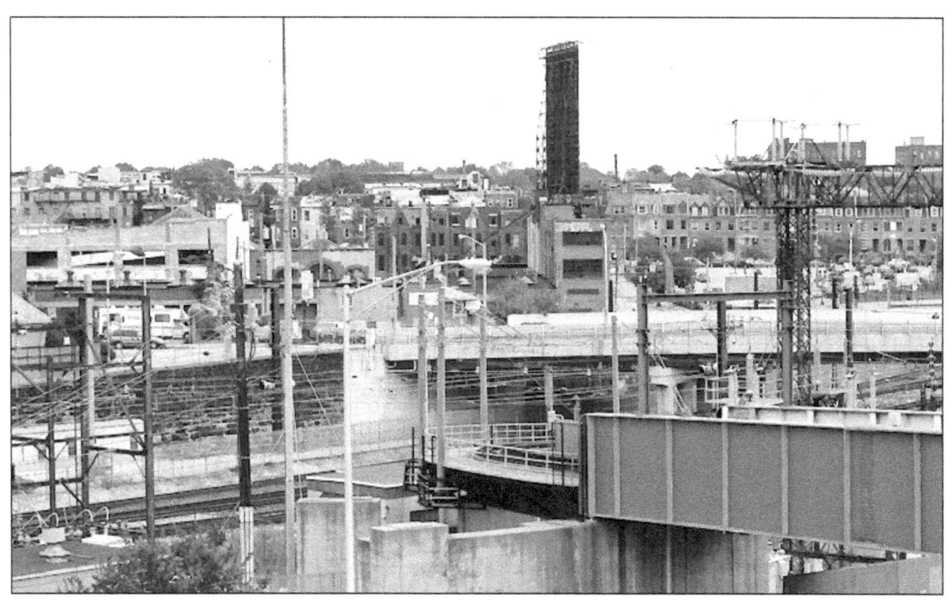

Lake Montebello
Mayfield

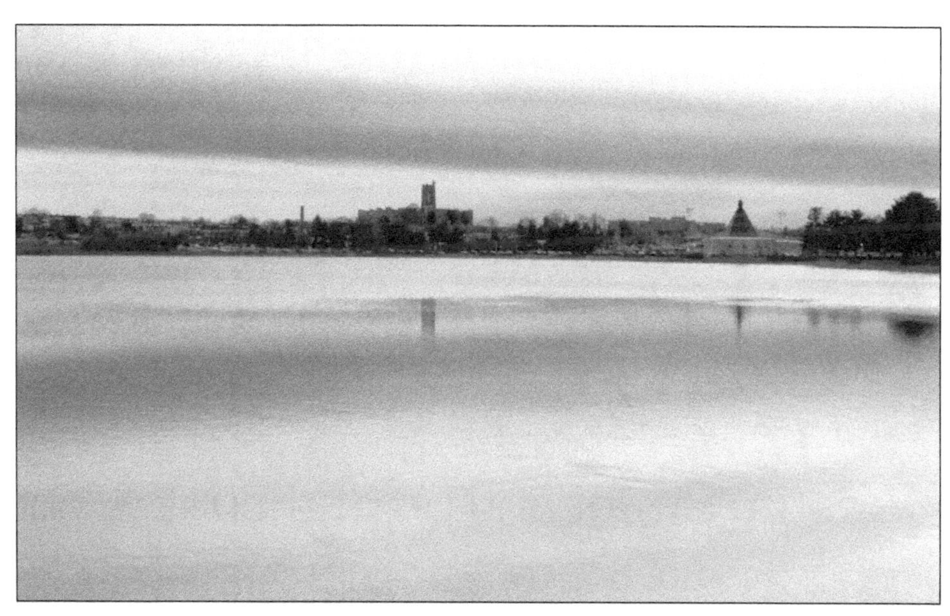

E. Preston Street and Greenmount Avenue
Johnston Square

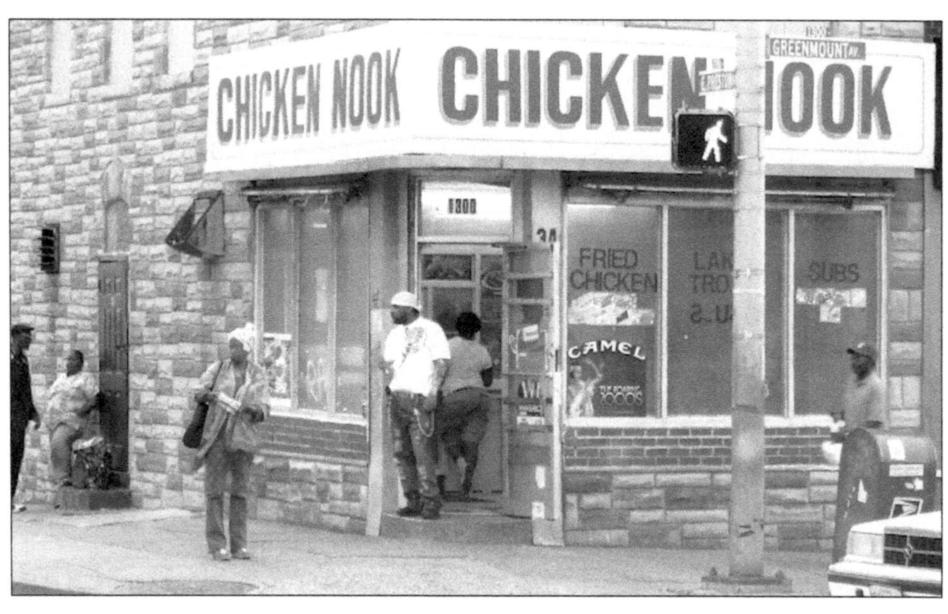
CHICKEN NOOK
CHICKEN
GREENMOUNT AV
FRIED CHICKEN
SUBS
CAMEL

W. Baltimore Street and Vincent Street
Franklin Square

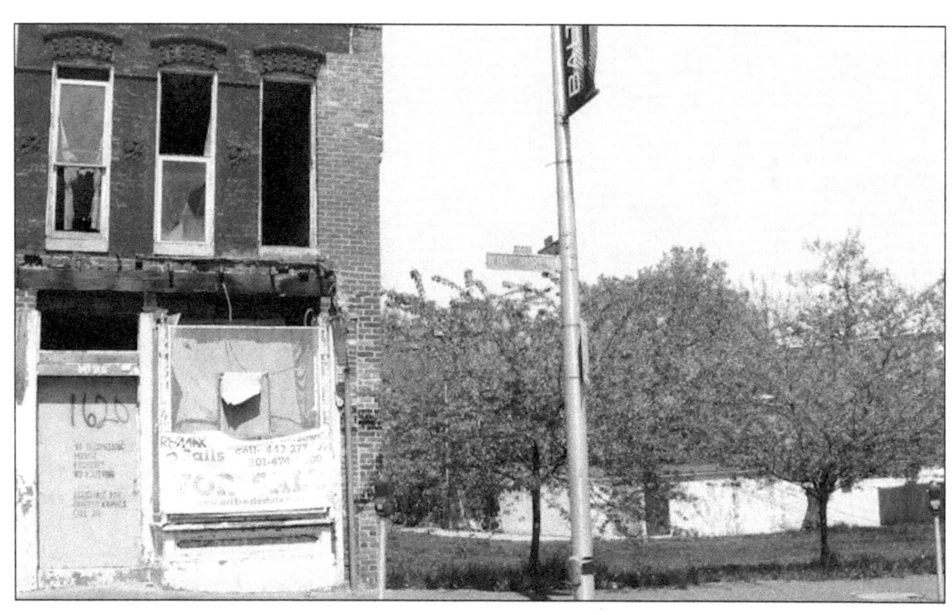
1620

E. Eager Street and Guilford Avenue
Midtown Belvedere

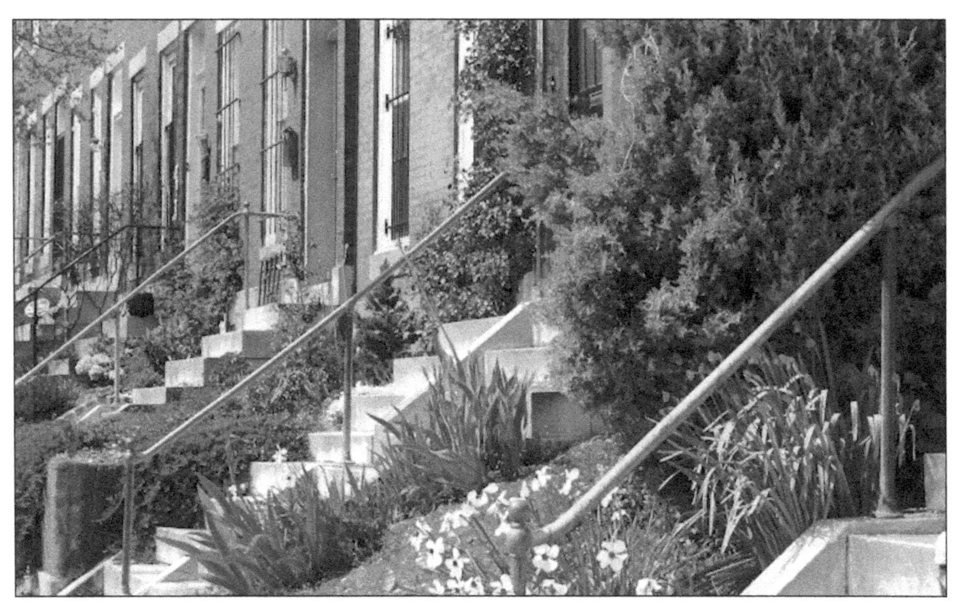

Mt. Royal Avenue and Oliver Street
Bolton Hill

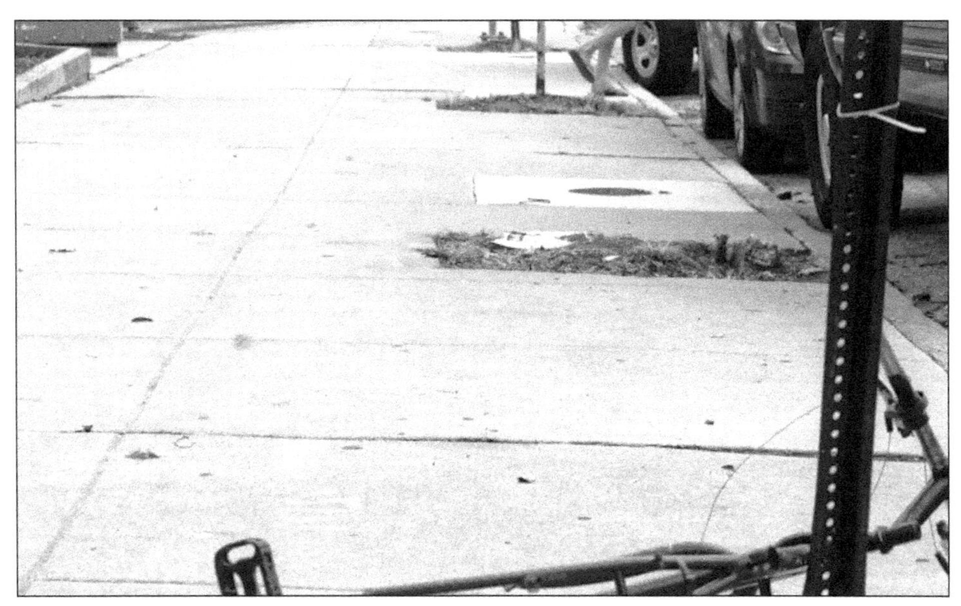

N. Chester Street and Ashland Avenue
Middle East

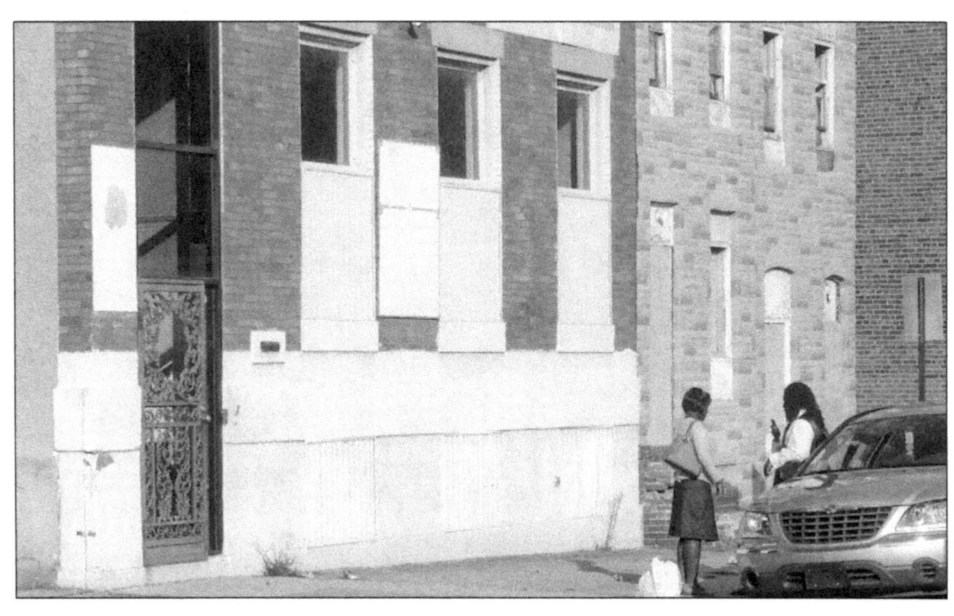

Mt. Royal Avenue and St. Paul Street
Midtown Belvedere

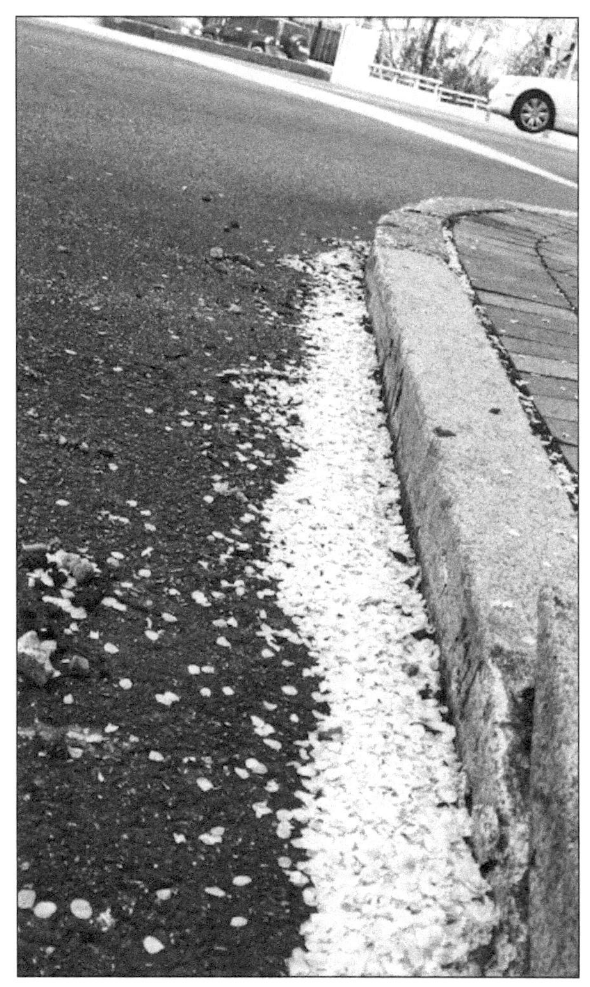

Westport Street and Maisel Street
Westport

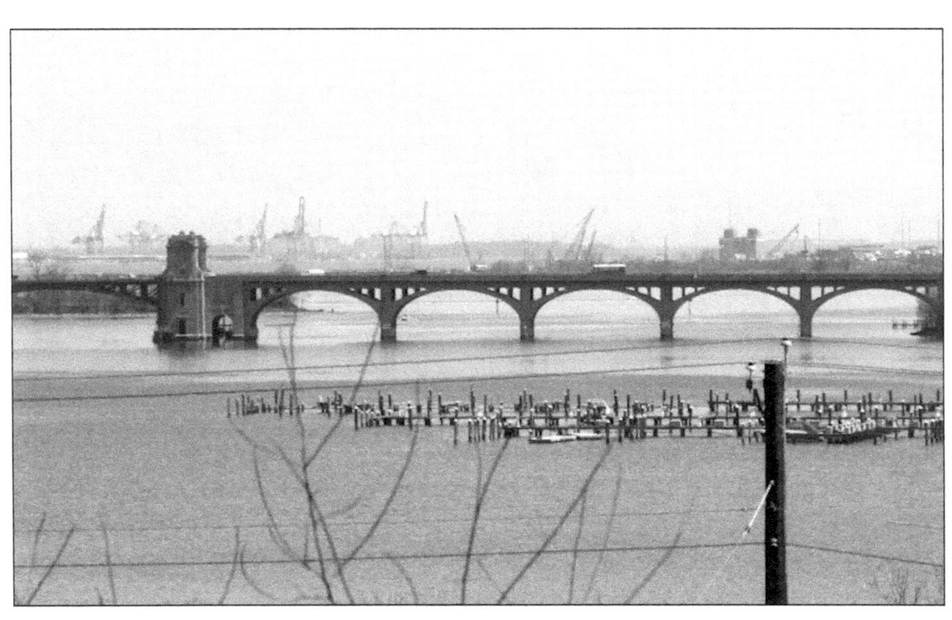

Lake Drive
Mayfield

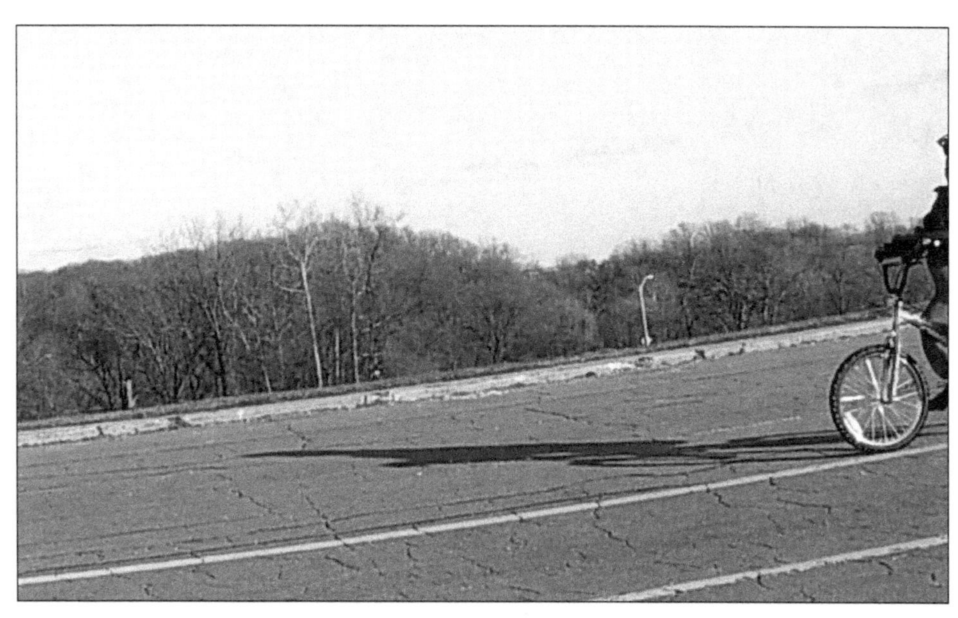

Lake Montebello

Mayfield

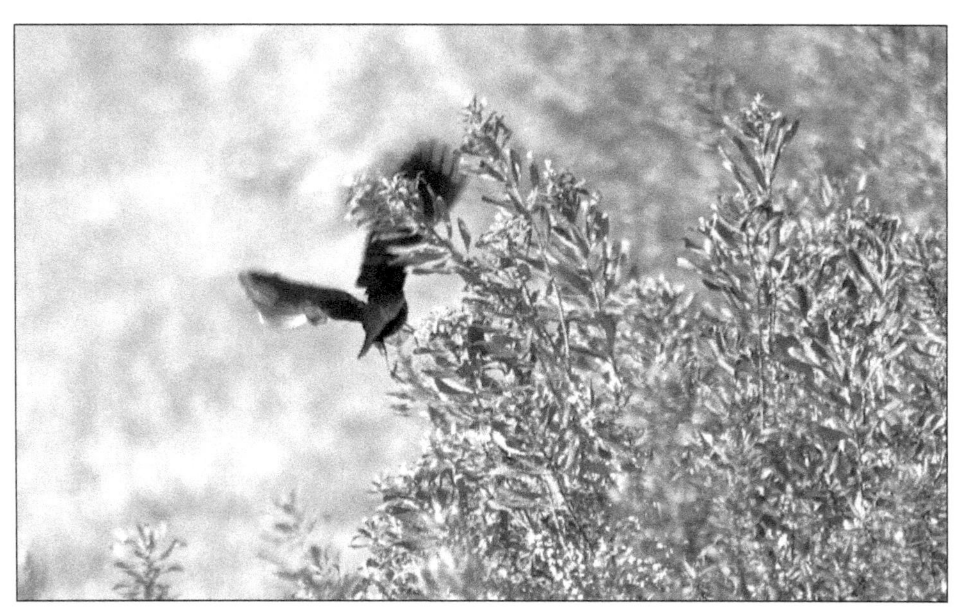

E. North Avenue and N. Rose Street
Berea

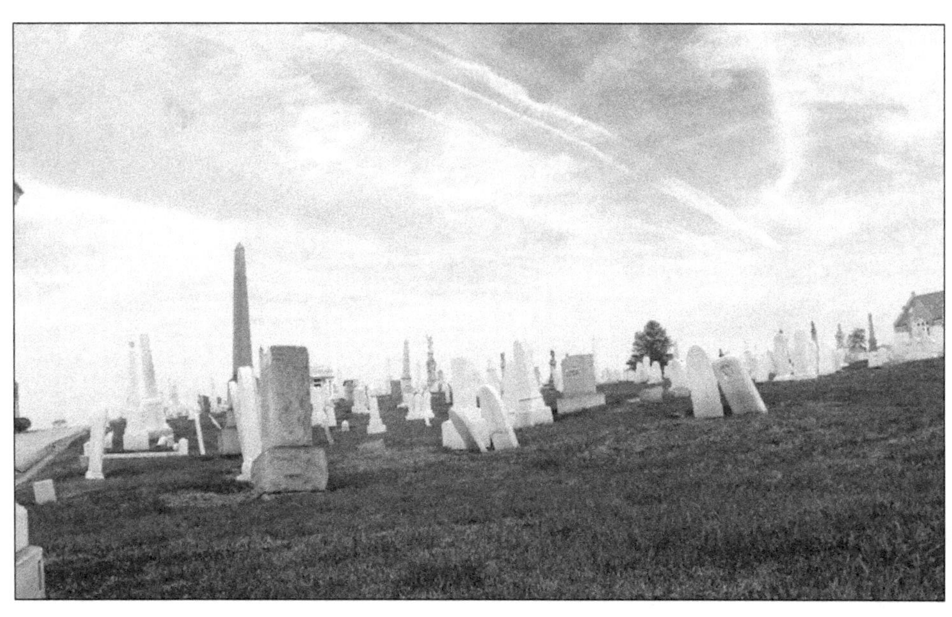

Hollins Street and S. Mount Street

Hollins Market

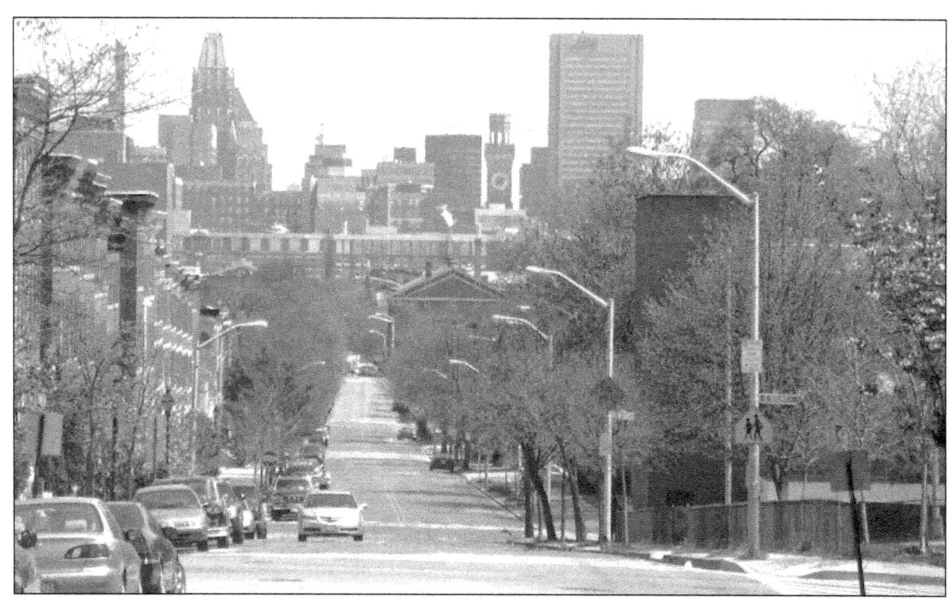

Russell Street and Haines Street

Gwynns Falls Trail

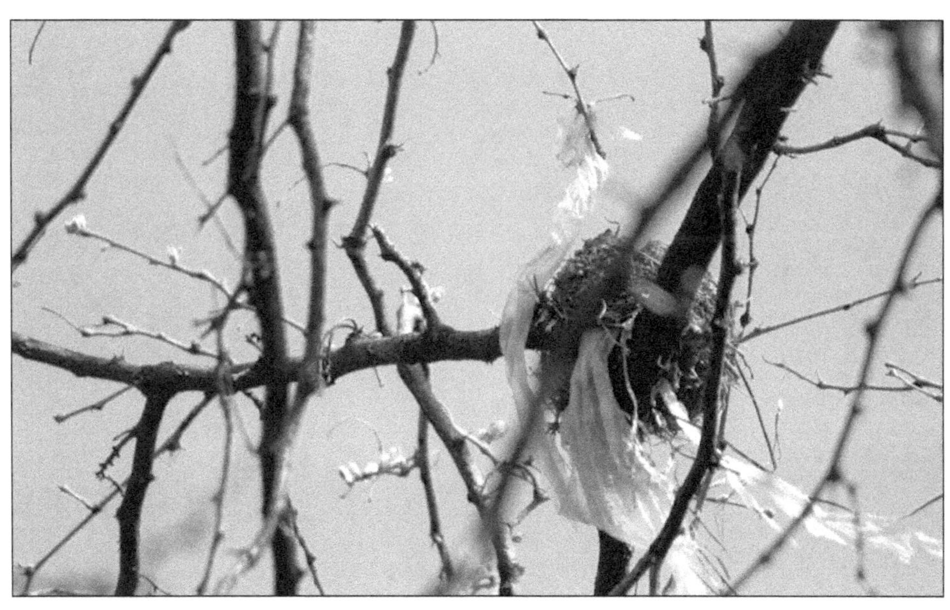

Harford Road and The Alameda

Coldstream-Homestead

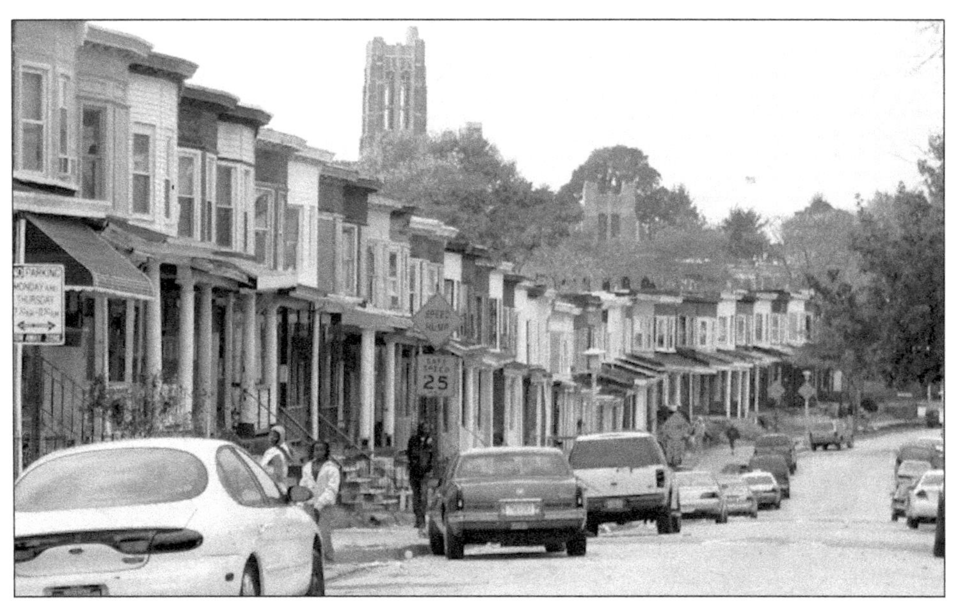
PARKING
MONDAY AND
THURSDAY
25

Maryland Avenue and W. Lanvale Street
Station North

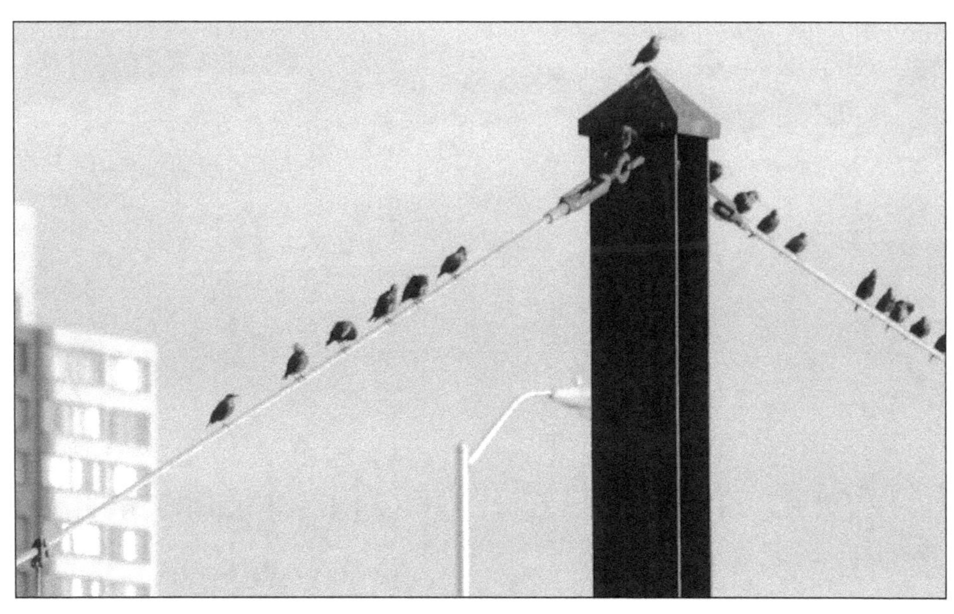

E. Monument Street and N. Charles Street
Mt. Vernon Square

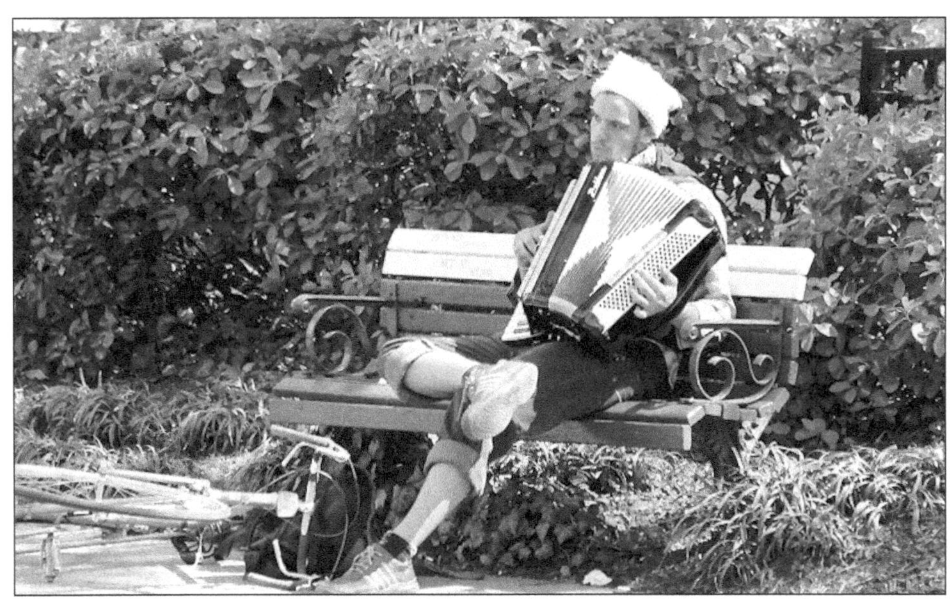

Mill Race Road

Hampden

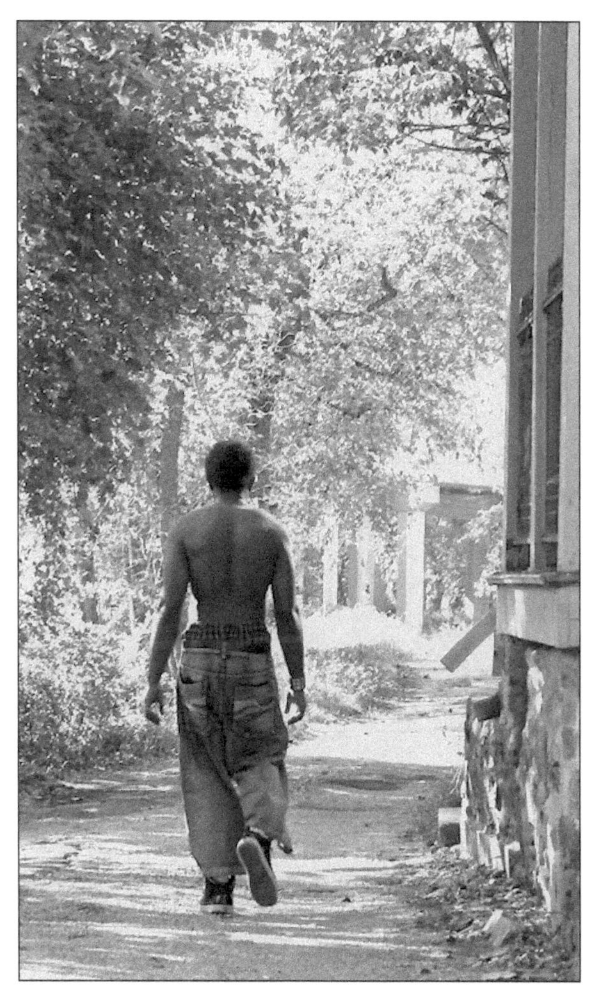

Notes

Particulars, holy and minute; page 33 — inspired by William Blake's advice, "Honor the particulars, holy and minute."

The soft hum of these bugs; page 35 — quotes George Oppen's poem, "Sympathy."

Sirens gust beyond the rooftops; page 41 — concludes with lines from Ted Nordhaus and Edward Shullenberger's book, *Breakthrough: The Death of Environmentalism and the Politics of Possibility*.

My eyes look everywhere; page 45 — contians a line inspired by Amy Lowell's poem, "Towns in Color" and quotes a line from James Wright's poem, "A Presentation of Two Birds to My Son."

The world outside the body is large; page 81 — contains a line from Rainer Maria Rilke's *Notebooks of Malte Laurids Brigges*.

Many of the lesser things have been told; page 85 — quotes Maya Angelou.

I study the lake's light; page 89 — quotes Paul Cezanne.

I never get tired; page 95 — draws from Tomas Tranströmer's poem, "Preludes."

[. . .]

It can be solved by walking; page 97 — inspired by the medieval Christian practice of pilgrimage and meditation, *solvitar ambulando*. The poem also quotes Frank O'Hara and Thomas Merton, and draws from a Nigerian folk tale re-told by Joseph Campbell in *The Power of Myth*.

There were people down in the depths; page 101 — an "updated" version of the many myths that explain the appearance of human beings.

We seek a form, a shape; page 103 — inspired by the work of the Baltimore artist Katherine Kavanaugh.

From within; page 109 — draws from lines found in Simone Weil's *First and Last Notebooks*.

Author's Note

The skies above Baltimore are filled with birds.
Pigeons, expected. Bald eagles, not. But they are there.
A red fox dashes from the golf course, across four traffic lanes, while shirtless boys play Frisbee on the university lawn, nicknamed, "The Beach."
The old gals on Hampden's porches dry their underwear in the back yard breezes.
West Baltimore's vacant lots steam with barbeque in empty oil drums. Stories, smoke and clouds — together in the air. An ecosystem of wishes and fears.

After my relocation from the lush suburbs north of Manhattan in 2001, I directed a short documentary film seeking to engage with Baltimore's citizens and their thoughts about nature. The project was a search for the place of trees and birds in a land of asphalt. In August 2009, after completing the edits, I scratched my head. How did it happen? For the two previous years, as I talked with people in the neighborhoods and wandered around town taking photos and video, I had shifted from poet, teacher, and editor to an earlier self: urban planner and naturalist. In that process I travelled further back — all the way to an adolescent fantasy: myself as a cross between Charles Darwin and Margaret Mead (Grace Slick was in there somewhere, too, but that's a different story). I had travelled far from the poet part of me.

[. . .]

A year after finishing the film, I found myself, thanks to a sabbatical from my teaching duties at the Maryland Institute College of Art, with six months of uninterrupted time. With mounds of field notes, interview transcripts, photographs and other scraps of musings, I wanted to develop the idea that the way we think of cities — geographical, cultural places — is too narrow. That they are ecological. That cities include all the components we typically associate with ecosystems: water, soil, flora, and fauna. But, as human places, cities also contain deeply embedded psychological/emotional materials: histories, memories, mythologies…a sort of psychoecology that might explain — on the cusp of humanity's projected 75% urban existence — our complex relationships with the natural world.

I planned a scholarly essay, something written for an academic conference in the social sciences. I settled in at my desk in a borrowed basement apartment in the Mayfield neighborhood of northeast Baltimore. But the material that had fit so nicely into the film wasn't "working." I couldn't feel a pulse. Somewhere deep in January's cold, something happened. It hit me like the silhouetted figure in Caspar David Friedrich's 19th century *Wanderer Above a Sea of Fog* (inset) — the exact image I needed if I wanted to know Baltimore.

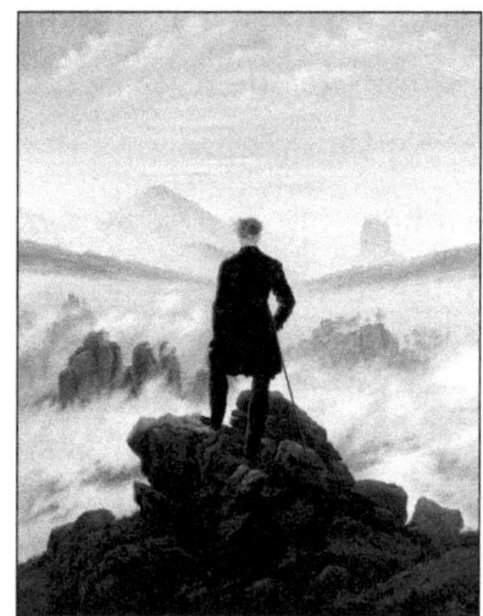

[. . .]

If I wanted to understand the nature of my new city, I would need Freidrich's lyric temperament. I would need to acknowledge within myself the obsessions of all the Romantic wanderers. I would need to return to poems…to their layered song and mystery. And, because poems are built with sensual language, and are "of the body," I would descend, as I have always thought Friedrich's wanderer needed to descend, from my cerebral mountaintop.

After I made the commitment to use poetry as a method of research as well as a mode of expression, something else happened. The form began to point me to myself as much as to the city I sought to understand. There came a sort of merging: the nature of the city, nature in the city, and my own nature. My historical and mythological nature was aroused in this place and by this place. Poetry was at work, subversive as ever, and taut with knowing what can't be known. I am reminded of Plato's Meno, who asked, "How do I go about finding the thing the nature of which is unknown to me?"

In my case, it was solved by poems…and by walking. I would not stand on some craggy mountaintop sublime. I became a pedestrian, continuing the practice of walking Baltimore's many neighborhoods. I punctuated my walks with additional field notes and photographs. Soon after, a photograph helped a poem to emerge. As the eye of my heart was opened by the poems, more photographs. And so on, an unlimited exchange between the two produced in my mind a sort of textile. A hypothesis, a proposal, a questioning, a witnessing, and a reaching for

[. . .]

the deep mythic stories that in humanity's cultural traditions weave the "beingness" of all things.

As James Agee reminded me more than once, "In the immediate world, everything is to be discerned…with the whole of consciousness, seeking to perceive it as it stands: so that the aspect of a street in sunlight can roar in the heart of itself as a symphony, perhaps as no symphony can: and all consciousness is shifted from the imagined…to the effort to perceive simply the cruel radiance of what is."

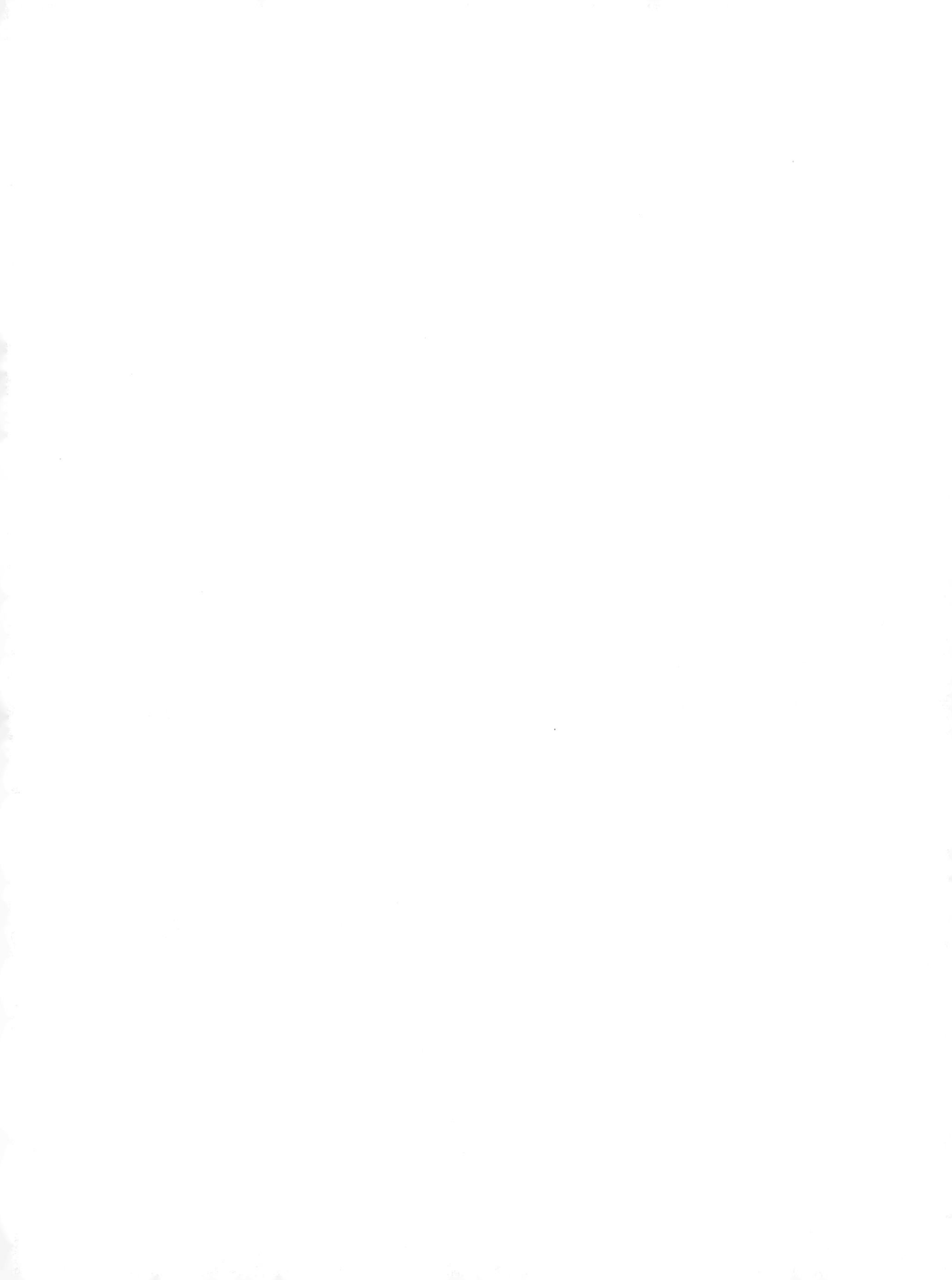

Acknowledgments

Grateful acknowledgment is made to the following journals in which poems, sometimes in slightly different forms, first appeared:

...a place wedged between	*Same River Twice*
At the intersection: burnt August fields	*Barrow Street*
City roofs at night under snow	*Georgetown Review*
From within	terrain.org
I study the lake's light	*The Penwood Review*
I wanted to change my name	terrain.org
In love	BaltimoreFishbowl.com
Inventory	*Same River Twice*
It can be solved by walking	Baltimore Fishbowl.com
Particulars, holy and minute	*The Potomac Review*
When the orange disc hoists itself	*Plainsongs*
From within	First published in the chapbook, *Minor Heaven*, by Toadlily Press (2005) in the anthology, *Desire Path*
Reliable as weather, the corner	Published in *The Best of Toadlily Press* (2011)

[. . .]

With gratitude to the Maryland Institute College of Art and Sarah Lawrence College for the gifts of time and space. So many people inspired me while at work on this project. Among them are: Linda Bills, Betsy Boyd, Anna Catone, Suzanne Garrigues, Victoria Givotovsky, Kate Knapp Johnson, Katherine Kavanaugh, Eve Andrée Laramée, Lia Purpura, residents (leaved, winged, and footed) of Baltimore City, Michael Salcman, Benjamin Shipley, Allen Strous, Jean Valentine, Kay and Jim Wallace, and especially my incomparable sons: Brian and Daniel Wallace. And, forever, Judy Remmel.

About the Author

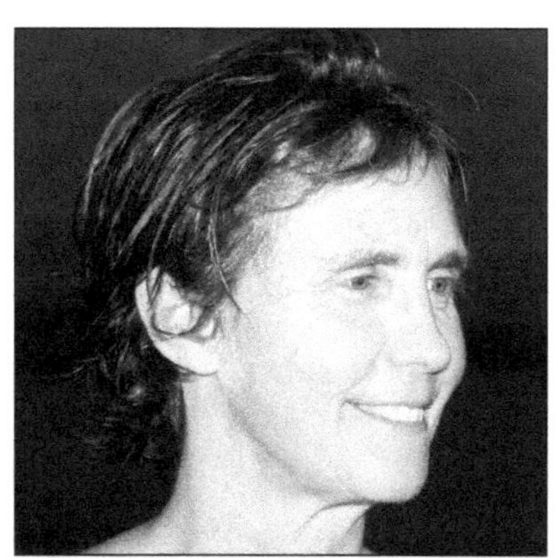

Jennifer Wallace teaches at the Maryland Institute College of Art in Baltimore, Maryland. She is a poetry editor at *The Cortland Review* and a founding editor of Toadlily Press. Her chapbook, *Minor Heaven*, appears in *Desire Path* (Toadlily Press, 2005). In 2009 she directed a short documentary, *Inter : View, A Conversation About Nature and the City*.

Jennifer's photographs have been exhibited at the Baltimore Museum of Art and at the Maryland Institute College of Art. She has written essays for exhibition catalogs and literary magazines; her poems appear in numerous journals and anthologies.

CityLit Press's mission is to provide a venue for writers who might otherwise be overlooked by larger publishers due to the literary nature or regional focus of their projects. It is the imprint of nonprofit CityLit Project, founded in Baltimore in 2004.

CityLit Project builds enthusiasm for the literary arts in the Baltimore metropolitan area and across Maryland for the benefit of readers, writers, and diverse audiences of all ages. It presents public festivals, author events, writers workshops, and programs for youth and seniors. It launched the CityLit Press imprint in 2010.

Thank you to major supporters: the National Endowment for the Arts, Maryland State Arts Council, the Baltimore Office of Promotion and The Arts, and the Baltimore Community Foundation. More information and documentation is available at www.guidestar.org.

Additional support is provided by individual contributors. Financial support is vital for sustaining the ongoing work of the organization. Secure, on-line donations can by made at www.citylitproject.org (click on "Donate").

CityLit is a member of Maryland Citizens for the Arts, the Greater Baltimore Cultural Alliance, the Maryland Association of Nonprofit Organizations, and the Writers' Conferences and Centers division of the Association of Writers and Writing Programs (AWP).

CityLit Project's offices are located in the School of Communications Design at the University of Baltimore.

www.ingramcontent.com/pod-product-compliance
Lightning Source LLC
LaVergne TN
LVHW080331110826
845155LV00024B/144

* 9 7 8 1 9 3 6 3 2 8 0 5 5 *